Contents

2	Ordering numbers	26	Angles in triangles
4	Addition and subtraction	28	Volume
6	Multiples and factors	30	Area and perimeter
8	Long multiplication	32	Polygons
10	Division	34	Circles
12	Problem solving	36	3D shapes
14	Fractions	38	Coordinates
16	Decimals	40	Statistics
18	Percentages	42	Quick test
20	Ratio and proportion	44	Explorer's logbook
22	Algebra	46	Answers
24	Standard measures		

Introduction

If you are wild about learning and wild about animals, this book is for you! It will take you on an adventure, where you will practise key maths skills and explore the amazing world of woodland animals along the way.

Each maths topic is introduced in a clear and simple way, with lots of interesting activities to complete, so that you can practise what you have learned.

You should attempt the tasks without a calculator unless instructed otherwise, but calculators may be used to check your answers.

Alongside every maths topic, you will discover fascinating facts about woodland creatures. The animals in this hugely diverse group live in the leafy ecosystems of temperate climates. What is your favourite woodland creature?

When you have completed each topic, record the animals that you have seen and the skills that you have learned in the explorer's logbook on pages 44–45.

Good luck, explorer! Try not to get too muddy!

Ordering numbers

Scientists **order** and classify animals according to their characteristics. Ordering animals helps us to understand and compare them. Numbers can also be **ordered** and compared depending upon the size of the digits and their place in the abacus.

Task 1 Write these numbers in words.

a 6 404 320 _six million Four hundred and Four thousand three Hundred and twenty_

b 9 000 015 _nine million and Fifteen_

Write these numbers in figures.

c ten million _10000000_

d five million and two _5000002_

Task 2 Order these numbers from the largest to the smallest.

a ~~3 444 004~~   ~~4 034 003~~   ~~4 033 999~~   ~~3 434 777~~   ~~4 300 990~~

_4,300,990 / 4,034,003 / 4,033,999 / 3,444,004 / 3,434,777_

b ~~−9~~   ~~−8~~   ~~−1~~   ~~4~~   ~~−2~~

_8, 4, −1, −2, −9_

Task 3   What is the value in words of the underlined 1 in these numbers?

a 1̲0 000 000   *ten million*

b 7 0̲10 398   *ten thousand*

c 8 473 1̲09   *one hundred*

d 5 271̲ 769   *one thousand*

e 9 1̲83 652   *one Hundred thousand*

f 8 222 331̲   *one*

WILD FACT

The red deer is Britain's largest land mammal. Males are called stags and females are called hinds.

Exploring Further ...

Put the answers to these questions into the abacus.

The numbers in the shaded squares correspond to letters based on their position in the alphabet. For example:
1 = A, 2 = B, 13 = M, 18 = R, etc.

Put the letters in the final column and rearrange to reveal an animal.

		M	HTh	TTh	Th	H	T	U
a	Write two million fifty-six thousand and seventy in figures.	B	E	N	O	O	O	O
b	Add 20 to −2.							
c	Round 35459 to the nearest 10000.							
d	Round 3 600 000 to the nearest million.							
e	What is the difference between −9 and 9?							
f	Add 10 000 to 490 000.							
g	Take 100 000 from 4 059 681.							

h   What animal did you discover? _____

Now canter to pages 44–45 to record what you have learned in your explorer's logbook.

Addition and subtraction

Migrating is second nature to a swallow. **Addition** and **subtraction** need to be second nature to us and, when problem solving, we have to recognise which **operations** and **methods** to use and why. First of all, investigate your mental skills. Next check out the written methods and then see if you can apply your knowledge and skills to problem solving.

FACT FILE

Animal: Swallow

Habitat: Open pasture with access to water and quiet farm buildings

Weight: 16 to 25g

Lifespan: Up to 4 years

Diet: Low-flying, large insects

Task 1	Complete these tasks mentally.

a Find the sum of 18901 and 1047. _19948_

b Add together 253573 and 436016. _689589_

c Find the difference between 6631 and 8972. _2341_

d Subtract 465230 from 697895. _232665_

Task 2   Complete these tasks mentally.

a Increase 2357 by 89.   _2446_

b What is 29 872 plus 228?   _1100_

c 34 871 – [6302] = 28 769

d 150 852 – [102 862] = 47 990 + 10

WILD FACT
Every autumn the swallow makes a journey of about 8000 miles to South Africa and then, every spring, it returns to Britain. It has to contend with very difficult conditions along the way.

Task 3   Complete these tasks using the columnar method.

a 35 491 + 57 273 + 4155
```
 57273
  4155
 96919
```
96919

b 783 029 + 18 942 + 305 823
```
783029
 18942
107794
```
1107794

c 101 063 – 87 452
```
 101063
 -87452
  13611
```
13611

d 965 256 – 778 373
```
 965256
 778373
 186883
```
186883

Exploring Further ...

One million eight hundred and seventy-five swallows left their winter feeding grounds in South Africa to spend summer in Europe. 46 257 died from a lack of food, 57 889 died because of poor weather conditions and a further nineteen thousand and five birds died from other causes. How many birds arrived safely?

_____

Check your answer by rounding all the figures to the nearest ten thousand.

Now swoop to pages 44–45 to record what you have learned in your explorer's logbook.

Multiples and factors

You should by now be really savvy about the properties of numbers from 1 to 100.

Multiples are 'sets of.'

9, 18, 27 and 36 are multiples or sets of 9.

Factors are the numbers which will divide into another number.

1, 2, 3, 6, 9 and 18 will all divide into 18, so they are all factors of 18.

A **prime number** is greater than 1 and will only divide by 1 and itself.

WILD FACT

Take care! The adder's bite does need medical attention! It is Britain's only venomous snake but, thankfully, in an encounter with humans it is more likely to flee than bite.

Task 1

Write down the next three multiples of these numbers.

a i) 4 __8__ __12__ __16__ **ii)** 40 __80__ __120__ __160__ **iii)** 400 ~~800~~ *800* __1200__ __1600__

b i) 11 __22__ __33__ __44__ **ii)** 110 __220__ __330__ __440__ **iii)** 1100 __2200__ __3300__ __4400__

c i) 7 __14__ __21__ __28__ **ii)** 70 __140__ __210__ __280__ **iii)** 700 __1400__ __2100__ __2800__

Task 2 Circle the factors of these two numbers.

a

72

② ③ 4 5 6 7 ⑧ ⑨ 10
11 ⑫ 14 15 16 17 18 ㉔ 36

b

42

② ③ 4 5 ⑥ 7 8 9 10
11 12 13 ⑭ 15 16 18 20 21

c What factors are missing for each number?

72 _____   42 _____

Task 3 Circle the factors common to these numbers: 35, 56, 91

a ① 3 5 ⑦ 8 13

What is the biggest number which will divide into all three of these numbers?

b 320, 360, 400 ___20___   **c** 560, 720, 960 ___20___

Exploring Further ...

a Test each number's divisibility by numbers 2–9 to discover which of them are prime numbers.

3, 13, 23, 33, 43, 53, 63, 73, 83, 93, 103, 113, 123, 133, 143, 153

_____

b If the number is **not** prime, state its lowest factor above 1.

_____

_____

Now slither to pages 44–45 to record what you have learned in your explorer's logbook.

Long multiplication

Long multiplication helps you to multiply numbers beyond the boundaries of the normal times tables. If you needed to multiply 592 by 67, you wouldn't be expected to know your 67 times table, but you can multiply by 7 and by 60 (6 × 10).

$$
\begin{array}{r}
592 \\
\times\ 67 \\
\hline
4144 \quad \times 7 \\
35520 \quad \times 10\ \times 6 \\
\hline
39664 \quad \times 7 + (\times 10\ \times 6) = \times 67
\end{array}
$$

Inserting the nought (zero) ensures you multiply by 10.

FACT FILE

Animal: Red fox
Habitat: Woodlands, rural and suburban environments
Weight: 3 to 11 kg
Lifespan: Up to 5 years
Diet: Rodents, rabbits, birds, game, fish, fruit, vegetables (and even rubbish!)

Task 1

Multiply by 10 by moving all the digits one place to the left and inserting a zero as the place holder:

54 ⟶ 540

a 69 _____   b 28 _____

c 179 _____   d 361 _____

Task 2

Multiply by multiples of 10:

$$
\begin{array}{r}
31 \\
\times\ 40 \\
\hline
1240 \quad \times 10\ \text{then}\ \times 4
\end{array}
$$

a 48
×70
_____

b 59
×30
_____

c 293
× 20
_____

d 706
× 90
_____

Task 3 Use long multiplication to calculate answers to these sums.

a 93 × 65

b 79 × 26

c 252 × 73

d 850 × 35

e 2910 × 19

f 5802 × 46

Task 4 Use rounding to estimate the answers to these sums.

a 82 × 67

b 27 × 25

c 31 × 54

d 429 × 75

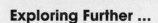

Exploring Further ...

A conservationist identifies 48 sites in a forest for tree planting. On each site he will plant 2875 conifer trees. He identifies a further 52 sites, on each of which he will plant 3485 trees. How many trees will he plant altogether?

a Before finding the exact number, underline the most efficient mental calculation that would give a sensible estimate.

(2880 × 50) + (3490 × 50)

(3000 × 50) + (3000 × 50)

(3000 × 50) + (3500 × 50)

(2900 × 50) + (3500 × 50)

b Now calculate the exact number. _____

Now scurry to pages 44–45 to record what you have learned in your explorer's logbook.

Division

You should be familiar with **long** and **short division**. Make sure you know how to deal with remainders using these methods.

WHOLE NUMBER REMAINDER	REMAINDER AS A FRACTION	REMAINDER AS A DECIMAL
$\dfrac{139}{5\overline{)697}}$ r2	$\dfrac{139}{5\overline{)697}}\ \frac{2}{5}$	$\dfrac{139.4}{5\overline{)697.^20}}$

Task 1

Divide by 10 by moving all the digits one place to the right:

450 ⟶ 45

a 960 _____   b 820 _____

c 9710 _____   d 1630 _____

Task 2

Fly through this task by dividing by multiples of 10.

a 540 ÷ 90 _____

b 560 ÷ 70 _____

c 480 ÷ 80 _____

d 650 ÷ 50 _____

FACT FILE

Animal:	Hen harrier
Habitat:	Open areas with low vegetation
Weight:	290 to 400 g
Lifespan:	Up to 7 years
Diet:	Voles, rats, grouse and squirrels

Task 3   Complete these using short division, showing the remainder as: i) a whole number, ii) a fraction, iii) a decimal.

a 7859 ÷ 5   b 9387 ÷ 4   c 9674 ÷ 8

i) _____   i) _____   i) _____

ii) _____   ii) _____   ii) _____

iii) _____   iii) _____   iii) _____

Task 4   Complete these calculations using long division.

Show the remainder as a whole number.

a 8536 ÷ 78

Show the remainder as a fraction.

b 4680 ÷ 32

Exploring Further …

Jamaal puts his plants into trays which hold 27 plants. He has to transplant 9700 plants.

a   How many complete trays can he fill?   _____

b   How many more plants does he need to fill another tray?   _____

c   He can deliver 50 trays to his shop in one journey.

How many journeys does he need to make? _____

Now fly to pages 44–45 to record what you have learned in your explorer's logbook.

Problem solving

Which operations do you use to solve problems? There are only four operations to choose from – **addition**, **subtraction**, **multiplication** and **division**. Sometimes you will have to use more than one operation and sometimes you will need to use your knowledge of the order of operations to carry out calculations: (**BODMAS**: Brackets; Orders (e.g. powers); Division; Multiplication; Addition; Subtraction).

WILD FACT

When feeding a family of six or seven chicks, the parent birds must catch up to 100 fish each day.

FACT FILE

Animal: Kingfisher

Habitat: Near lakes, ponds, canals, streams and rivers of Europe, North Africa and Asia

Weight: 35 to 40 g

Lifespan: 5 to 7 years

Diet: Fish and aquatic insects

Task 1 Answer the following using BODMAS.

a $13 + 16 \div 2 =$

b $5 \times 3 + 2 \times 4 - 12 \div 4 =$

c $8 \times 3 + 9 \div 3 - 8 =$

d $35 - (15 + 5 \times 3) =$

Task 2 Use BODMAS to answer the following.

a $(4 + 2)^2 + 3 \times 2 - 2^2 =$

b $(12 \div 2 + 8) - (5^2 - 3 \times 7) =$

c $(4^2 + 2 - 6) \div (3^2 + 7 - 7 \times 2) =$

d $(3^3 \div 3 \times 2) - 2^3 =$

Task 3 — Work out these problems.

a The total length of four adders is 260 cm.
The total length of two of the adders is 143 cm.
The third adder measures 62 cm.
What is the length of the fourth adder?

_____

b The 2010 Hen Harrier Survey reported 617 breeding
pairs of hen harriers in the UK and a further 29 pairs on
the Isle of Man. In 2004 there were 770 breeding pairs
in the UK and a further 36 pairs on the Isle of Man.

Complete this sentence:

In the _____ years from 2004 to 2010, the total

number of hen harriers in the UK and the Isle

of Man fell by _____.

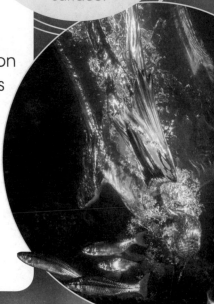

Task 4 — Now solve the following problems.

a A flock of swallows flies a total distance of 3902 km. The first leg was
359 km, the second leg was 451 km and the third leg was 1349 km.

What was the distance of the fourth leg of the journey? _____

b There were 57 swallows in the flock. What was the total

number of kilometres travelled by the whole flock? _____

Exploring Further ...

The total weight of three deer – a red deer, a fallow deer
and a roe deer – is 236 kg. The red deer is the heaviest and weighs
119 kg. The roe deer weighs 47 kg less than the fallow deer. Find out
the weights of the fallow and roe deer.

Fallow deer _____ Roe deer _____

**Now skim to pages 44–45 to record what you
have learned in your explorer's logbook.**

Fractions

WILD FACT

A wolf spider's eight eyes ensure that small insects do not stand a chance of passing by unnoticed.

FACT FILE

Animal: Wolf spider
Habitat: A range of inland and coastal habitats
Lifespan: Up to 2 years
Diet: Insects and invertebrates

Task 1 Simplify each fraction by finding the highest common factor.

a i) $\dfrac{9}{12}$ ii) $\dfrac{2}{20}$ iii) $\dfrac{8}{12}$ iv) $\dfrac{12}{18}$

b i) $\dfrac{25}{60}$ ii) $\dfrac{24}{33}$ iii) $\dfrac{35}{42}$ iv) $\dfrac{36}{81}$

Find the lowest denominator (lowest multiple) common to these fractions.

c $\dfrac{1}{8}$ $\dfrac{1}{3}$ $\dfrac{1}{12}$ _____   d $\dfrac{1}{7}$ $\dfrac{1}{6}$ $\dfrac{1}{3}$ _____

Task 2 Express these fractions with the same denominator, then order them from smallest to largest.

a $\dfrac{7}{8}$ $\dfrac{2}{3}$ $\dfrac{11}{12}$

b $\dfrac{13}{18}$ $\dfrac{5}{9}$ $\dfrac{7}{12}$

Task 3   Find the lowest common denominator for these fractions and add or subtract. Remember to simplify.

a i) $\dfrac{3}{4} + \dfrac{5}{16} =$ ii) $\dfrac{11}{15} + \dfrac{3}{5} =$

b i) $\dfrac{7}{10} - \dfrac{2}{5} =$ ii) $\dfrac{7}{18} - \dfrac{2}{12} =$

c i) $4\dfrac{4}{9} + 1\dfrac{1}{3} =$ ii) $3\dfrac{3}{4} + 4\dfrac{3}{14} =$

Task 4   You do not need a common denominator when multiplying fractions. Remember that **of** means × and always simplify where possible.

a i) $\dfrac{3}{5} \times \dfrac{1}{3} =$ ii) $\dfrac{2}{9} \times \dfrac{3}{8} =$

b i) $\dfrac{1}{4}$ of 24 =   ii) $\dfrac{4}{5}$ of 35 =

Dividing by 2 is the same as multiplying by $\frac{1}{2}$

c i) $\dfrac{1}{4} \div 2 =$ ii) $\dfrac{2}{7} \div 4 =$

WILD FACT

Unlike the majority of spiders, the wolf spider does not catch its food in a web. It tracks its prey, creeps up on it and then uses its speed to pounce.

Exploring Further ...

Draw a line of web to match a spider fraction to its equivalent insect fraction.

Now creep to pages 44–45 to record what you have learned in your explorer's logbook.

Decimals

Decimals can be written as fractions where the **denominator** is a power of ten and the **numerator** is expressed by the number(s) following the decimal point.

e.g. $0.8 = \frac{8}{10}$ $0.08 = \frac{8}{100}$ $0.008 = \frac{8}{1000}$

The **decimal point** separates the whole number from the parts.

e.g. 6.8 means 6 whole ones and 8 tenths of a whole one.

Task 1   Give the value of the **threes** in words.

a 3641.8   _____

b 7082.273   _____

c 53.4   _____

d 367.5   _____

FACT FILE

Animal: Spittle bug
Habitat: Woodland, grassland, meadows and gardens
Weight: Up to 12 mg
Lifespan: 5 to 6 months
Diet: Plant sap

Task 2   Work out the answers to the following.

a Multiply by 100.   i) 5.7 = _____   ii) 93.64 = _____

b Divide by 100.   i) 12.4 = _____   ii) 197.5 = _____

c Multiply by 1000.   i) 3.57 = _____   ii) 0.004 = _____

d Divide by 1000.   i) 507 = _____   ii) 81 529 = _____

Task 3 Calculate the decimal fraction equivalent to these fractions by dividing the numerator by the denominator.

a $\dfrac{17}{20}$ = _____   b $\dfrac{7}{8}$ = _____

Give your answer to 1, 2 or 3 dp, remembering to place a dot over the recurring number.

c $\dfrac{5}{9}$ = _____   d $\dfrac{7}{12}$ = _____

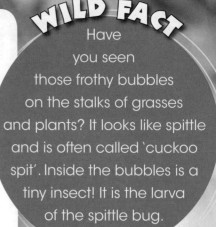

WILD FACT Have you seen those frothy bubbles on the stalks of grasses and plants? It looks like spittle and is often called 'cuckoo spit'. Inside the bubbles is a tiny insect! It is the larva of the spittle bug.

Task 4 Use a formal written method to answer these questions.

a 2.45 × 3   b 5.09 × 6

Show the remainder as a decimal.

c 24 ÷ 5   d 689 ÷ 4

WILD FACT The spittle is a mixture of watery waste, air and a glandular substance which the bug secretes through an abdominal hole.

Exploring Further ...

After completing some calculations on average numbers of spittle bugs around the Beckdale Reservoir, a scientist ended up with some complex figures. Help him to make these figures more manageable by rounding them to the nearest whole number.

Area 1: 37.4   _____

Area 2: 85.6   _____

Area 3: 23.79   _____

Area 4: 119.49 _____

Now scuttle to pages **44–45** to record what you have learned in your explorer's logbook.

Percentages

FACT FILE

Animal:	Red squirrel
Habitat:	Trees across Europe and Siberia
Weight:	275 to 300 g
Lifespan:	Up to 6 years
Diet:	Seeds, buds, flowers, shoots, nuts, berries, fungi, fruit and insects

Out of the estimated 2.65 million squirrels in the UK, 160 000 are red and 2.5 million are grey. Turning these figures into **percentages** makes them more meaningful! For example:

Just 6% of the squirrel population in the UK is red. The remaining 94% of the population is grey.

Discover how skilled you are with percentages.

Task 1 Change these percentages into fractions.

a 71% =

b 3% =

Change these percentages into fractions which are in their lowest terms.

c 25% =

d 50% =

Task 2 Change these percentages into decimals.

a 91% = _____

b 256% = _____

c 8% = _____

d 1% = _____

Change these decimals into percentages.

e 0.12 = _____

f 0.37 = _____

g 0.05 = _____

h 3.61 = _____

Task 3   Change these fractions into percentages.

a $\dfrac{99}{100}$ = _____   b $\dfrac{9}{100}$ = _____

c $\dfrac{4}{5}$ = _____   d $\dfrac{19}{20}$ = _____

Task 4   If you're still nuts about percentages, try these sums.

a Find 10% of: i) 40 = _____   ii) 160 = _____   iii) 380 = _____

b Find 5% of: i) 40 = _____   ii) 160 = _____   iii) 380 = _____

c Find 15% of: i) 40 = _____   ii) 160 = _____   iii) 380 = _____

Exploring Further ...

See how quickly you can complete this table.

Fraction	Percentage (%)	Decimal
$\dfrac{4}{5}$		
	25	
		0.3
	70	
$\dfrac{7}{20}$		
		0.52
		0.15
	82	
$\dfrac{1}{25}$		

A time of less than two minutes means you know all these facts by heart! Well done!

Now scamper to pages 44–45 to record what you have learned in your explorer's logbook.

Ratio and proportion

Ratio tells us how much we have of one thing **compared to** another.

A ratio of 6:2 here means that for every 6 red squares there are 2 blue ones.

If the ratio stays the same as the quantities increase or decrease, then they are in **proportion**. The two quantities will only remain in proportion if the increase or decrease occurs through × or ÷.

Task 1   A recipe for bird cake requires 6 grams of bird seed and 12 grams of suet.

a How many grams of seed are required for 24 grams of suet? _____

b How many grams of suet are required for 18 grams of seed? _____

Five packets of bird seed cost £4.50. What is the cost of:

c 10 packets? _____   **e** 15 packets? _____

d 1 packet? _____   **f** 3 packets? _____

Task 2 A map is drawn to a scale of 1 cm to 4 km. What length on the map stands for:

a 2 km? _____ b 8 km? _____ c 9 km? _____

7 cm on a map represents 280 km. What distance is represented by:

d 14 cm? _____ e 2 cm? _____ f 3 cm? _____

Task 3 On a bird-watching expedition, $\frac{1}{10}$ of the group are adults. There are 36 children.

a What fraction of the group are children?

b How many adults are in the group? _____

c How many people are there altogether? _____

d Write down the ratio of adults to children. _____

e What percentage of the people are adults? _____

f What percentage are children? _____

Exploring Further ...

I observed sparrows, starlings, blackbirds, wrens and robins in the ratio of 8:6:3:2:1 in my garden. I made 60 sightings in total. Complete the information in this table.

Type of Bird	Ratio Part	Actual Number Seen	Fraction over 60	Fraction in Lowest Terms	Percentage	Decimal Fraction
Sparrow	8					
Starling	6					
Blackbird	3					
Wren	2					
Robin	1					
TOTAL		60				

Now hop to pages 44–45 to record what you have learned in your explorer's logbook.

Algebra

Most of the maths you do involves finding an unknown amount or value. **Algebra** gives unknown values a name in the form of a letter or symbol.

So instead of writing: $6 + \square = 10$

We write: $6 + x = 10$

Start by getting used to missing numbers, then discover what fun working with letters can be.

FACT FILE

Animal: Pipistrelle bat

Habitat: Woodland, wetland, grassland, farms, parks and gardens across the UK and Europe

Weight: 3 to 9 g

Lifespan: 4 to 5 years

Diet: Small flying insects

Task 1

Write the next three numbers (terms) in these sequences.

a 46   42   38   34   ____   ____   ____

b   8   11   15   20   ____   ____   ____

c   7   5   3   1   ____   ____   ____

WILD FACT

The pipistrelle bat has a mouse-like, fur-covered body, soft leathery wings, pointy ears and sharp teeth.

Task 2

Write the missing numbers.

a _____   _____   _____   498   504   510

b −12   _____   _____   3   8   _____

What is the rule for these sequences?

c 691   592   493   394   295   196   _____

d 15   16   18   21   25   30

_____

Task 3 Find the value of the letter in these equations. Give your answer in the form '$x = ...$', '$m = ...$' and so on. Put your answer back into the equation to make sure it is correct.

a **i)** $12 + 46 = x$ _____ **ii)** $y + 23 = 45$ _____ **iii)** $18 + z = 39$ _____

b **i)** $56 - 32 = a$ _____ **ii)** $78 - b = 35$ _____ **iii)** $c - 42 = 65$ _____

c **i)** $6 \times 12 = p$ _____ **ii)** $q \times 8 = 56$ _____ **iii)** $9 \times r = 54$ _____

d **i)** $81 \div 9 = k$ _____ **ii)** $32 \div m = 16$ _____ **iii)** $n \div 7 = 6$ _____

Task 4 Give two possible values for each letter to satisfy these equations.

a $x + y = 11$ _____ _____

b $p \times q = 12$ _____ _____

Find the value of **c** in these equations when $a = 8$ and $b = 4$

c $a - b = c$ _____   **d** $a \div b = c$ _____

WILD FACT
A single pipistrelle can eat over 3000 insects in one night!

Exploring Further ...

We find how far someone or something has travelled (**distance**) by multiplying the **speed**, by the **time** taken. The formula for this is $D = S \times T$. To find the **speed**, you divide **distance** by **time**: $S = D \div T$ and to find **time** you divide **distance** by **speed** $T = D \div S$. Use these formulae to compare these speeds, times and distances.

	Distance (in metres)	Time (in minutes)	Speed (metres per minute)	Speed (kilometres per hour)
Red deer	2400	3		
Kingfisher		$1\frac{1}{2}$	600	
Swallow	600			54

Which animal is the fastest? _____

Now flit to pages 44–45 to record what you have learned in your explorer's logbook.

Standard measures

All the creatures on our planet can be measured. By knowing their lengths and weights, we can compare them. Do you know the facts for all the **standard measures**? And can you convert one to another with ease?

Task 1

Match these body lengths (they do not include the tail) and weights to the appropriate mammal.

0.71 kg	5.1 g	2.75 m	25 cm
120 kg	112 cm	50 mm	5.9 kg

		Length	Weight
a	Red deer	_____	_____
b	Harvest mouse	_____	_____
c	Red fox	_____	_____
d	Squirrel	_____	_____

WILD FACT

The way in which the harvest mouse builds its nest amongst tall grasses is a real feat of engineering! The female balances about 30 cm up a grass stem and weaves the leaves growing on that stem into a little basket-style nest. She then weaves more grasses into it to form a sphere about 8–10 cm in diameter.

Task 2   Explore the following questions.

a How many kg in 0.7 of a tonne? _____

b What is the value in cm of 0.1 of 8 metres? _____

c What decimal fraction of a tonne is 160 kg? _____

d Express 7500 ml as a decimal fraction of 25 litres. _____

e How many miles in 4.8 km? (1 mile = 1.6 km) _____

Task 3   It's time to answer the following questions!

a How many seconds in?

   i) 5.4 min _____   **ii)** 1.75 min _____

b How many days in?

   i) 3.5 weeks _____   **ii)** January and April _____

c What is 0.3 of an hour in minutes? _____

d How many minutes and seconds in 0.125 of an hour? _____

Exploring Further ...

James and Sadie went on a wildlife-spotting expedition but in their report about it they did not use sensible standard measures.

Can you make the figures in this report more meaningful?

We set off on a **i) 120 hour** _____ long expedition. The first day was spent getting to our destination, some **ii) 800 000 cm** _____ from home. It took us **iii) 14 400 seconds** _____. We were very excited to spot two animals. One was about **iv) 3000 mm** _____ in length and weighed about **v) 15 000 g** _____. It had a tail **vi) 0.4 m** _____ long. The second was tinier than a harvest mouse, just **vii) 0.004 kg** _____ in weight and measuring **viii) 0.04 m** _____.

Now scamper to pages 44–45 to record what you have learned in your explorer's logbook.

Angles in triangles

A **triangle** is the name given to a 2D shape with three sides and three angles. There are four types of triangle:

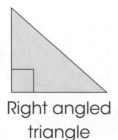

Right angled triangle

Equilateral triangle

Isosceles triangle

Scalene triangle

Task 1   State whether each of these statements about triangles is true or false.

a A triangle can have one obtuse angle.   _____

b A triangle can have two obtuse angles.   _____

c A triangle can have two right angles.   _____

d An equilateral triangle has three equal angles. _____

e An isosceles triangle has two equal angles.   _____

Task 2

The reception class are making templates for butterfly wings. Help the teacher by calculating the missing angles.

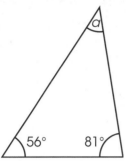 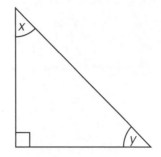 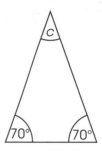

a Calculate the size of angle *a*. _____

b Two of the values below match *x* and *y*. Which are they?

42°   58°   62°   38°   48°   52°   _____   _____

c Calculate the size of angle *c*. _____

Task 3

State which type of triangle – right angled, equilateral, isosceles or scalene – matches each description.

a Angles measure 79°, 51° and 50°.   _____

b Sides measure 4 cm, 4 cm and 4 cm.   _____

c Two of the angles measure 73° and 17°. _____

d Two of the angles measure 34° and 34°. _____

Exploring Further ...

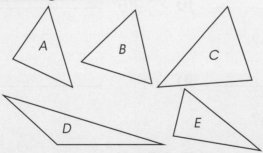

a Which is the equilateral triangle?_____

b What makes an equilateral triangle different from other triangles?

_____

_____

Now flutter to pages 44–45 to record what you have learned in your explorer's logbook.

WILD FACT

When the tortoiseshell butterfly is resting, it folds its wings up and is perfectly camouflaged as a leaf. If it is discovered by a bird, it flicks its wings open. The sudden flash of colour frightens the bird.

Volume

Volume is a measure which deals with three-dimensional (3D) shapes. Volume tells us how much space there is inside a container – how much it will hold. Because three dimensions are involved, the answer is always given in cube units: mm^3, cm^3, m^3 and km^3.

Animal: Scottish wildcat
Habitat: Woodland and large grassland areas of the Scottish Highlands
Weight: 5 to 8 kg
Lifespan: 10 to 12 years
Diet: Rabbits, rats, hares and other small mammals

Task 1   Answer the following questions.

a How many mm^3 are there in?

i) $2\,cm^3$ _____   ii) $3.5\,cm^3$ _____

b How many cm^3 are there in?

i) $4000\,mm^3$_____   ii) $1\,m^3$ _____

c How many cm^3 are there in?

i) $4\,m^3$ _____   ii) $2.5\,m^3$ _____

d How many m^3 are there in?

i) $3\,000\,000\,cm^3$ _____   ii) $1\,500\,000\,cm^3$ _____

Task 2   Find the volume of these cuboids.

a   6 cm × 4 cm × 2 cm   _____   b   5 m × 3 m × 4 m   _____

c   7 mm × 8 mm × 2 mm   _____   d   5 cm × 4 cm × 6 cm   _____

e   3 m × 2 m × 8 m   _____   f   4 mm × 5 mm × 8 mm   _____

Task 3   Make a rough sketch on a piece of paper and write on the dimensions to help you.

a   A cuboid measures 6 cm × 4 cm × 3 cm.

   i)   What is the area of each of its faces?

   _____   _____   _____

   ii)   What is its volume?   _____

b   A model is made from 1 cm cubes. It measures 12 cm × 5 cm × 4 cm. It weighs 7.2 kg. What is the weight of each 1 cm cube in grams?

   _____

c   A cubic metre of water weighs 1000 kg. A cubic metre holds 1000 litres of water. A tank full of water weighs 221 000 kg. The tank measures 4 m × 6 m × 9 m.

   i)   What is the weight of the tank when empty?

   _____

   ii)   How many litres of water does the tank hold?

   _____

WILD FACT

Did you know that a wildcat is an actual breed of cat and not just a cat which is living in the wild? The wildcat is a cousin of our domestic cats.

WILD FACT

The wildcat is one of the UK's rarest mammals, found only in the remotest parts of the countryside.

Exploring Further ...

A school is producing pamphlets on protecting the wildcat. Small boxes of the pamphlets measuring 15 cm × 5 cm × 4 cm are packed into large boxes measuring 60 cm × 20 cm × 16 cm. One-quarter of the volume of the large box is left for extra packing.

How many small boxes of pamphlets are in each large box? _____

Now prowl to pages 44–45 to record what you have learned in your explorer's logbook.

Area and perimeter

You should be familiar with the **area** of **rectangles** and **squares** by now. Now investigate what you know about the area of **triangles** and **parallelograms**.
Remember:

Area of triangle $= \frac{1}{2}\left(\text{base} \times \dfrac{\text{perpendicular}}{\text{height}}\right)$

Area of parallelogram $= \text{base} \times \dfrac{\text{perpendicular}}{\text{height}}$

FACT FILE

Animal: Hare
Habitat: Open farmland
Weight: 4 to 6 kg
Lifespan: 4 to 12 years
Diet: Grasses, herbs, cereal crops, buds, twigs and tree bark

Task 1 What is the i) area and ii) perimeter of:

a a rectangle 5 m × 4 m?

   i) _____ **ii)** _____

b a square with sides of 5 cm?

   i) _____ **ii)** _____

c a rectangle 153 m by 34 m?

   i) _____ **ii)** _____

d a square with sides of 8 m?

   i) _____ **ii)** _____

e a rectangle 6 cm × 12 cm?

   i) _____ **ii)** _____

f a square with sides of 24 mm?

   i) _____ **ii)** _____

Task 2

Two rectangular cards 4 cm by 12 cm are rearranged into the pattern shown.

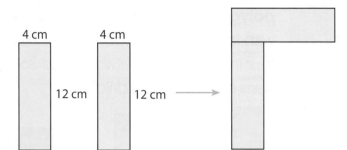

4 cm   4 cm

12 cm   12 cm

Calculate the area and perimeter of the new shape.

A: _____   P: _____

Task 3

Explore these area problems.

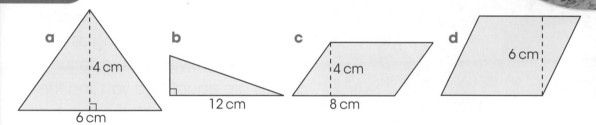

a

4 cm

6 cm

b

12 cm

c

4 cm

8 cm

d

6 cm

Find the area of triangle **a**. _____

The area of triangle **b** is 18 cm². What is its height? _____

Find the area of parallelogram **c**. _____

The area of parallelogram **d** is 54 cm².

What is the length of its base? _____

Exploring Further ...

Side *a* is twice the length of side *b*.

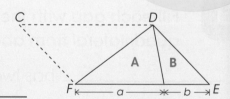

a What can you discover about the areas of triangles A and B?

_____

_____

b What can you discover about the area of parallelogram *CDEF*?

_____

_____

Now dart to pages 44–45 to record what you have learned in your explorer's logbook.

31

Polygons

Any 2D shape with straight sides is a **polygon**. A **quadrilateral** is a polygon with four sides and four angles. The four interior angles always total 360°. Here are some quadrilaterals:

Square   Rectangle   Parallelogram

Rhombus   Trapezium   Kite

Polygons also have exterior angles. The sum of the exterior angles is 360°. In a regular polygon the exterior angles are equal and you find their size by dividing 360 by the number of sides, e.g. the exterior angle of a regular hexagon is
$360 \div 6 = 60°$.

60°

FACT FILE

Animal:	Honey bee / Bumble bee
Habitat:	Meadows and gardens
Weight:	0.04 to 0.60 g
Lifespan:	4 weeks to 4 months depending on the job of the bee (queen honey bees live up to 4 years)
Diet:	Nectar and pollen

WILD FACT

Unlike its cousin the honey bee, a bumble bee does not die when it uses its sting. The males do not have a sting at all and the female will not sting unless under threat.

Task 1 Fill each gap with the name of a quadrilateral from above.

a A _____ has two pairs of adjacent sides which are equal.

b A _____ has four equal sides and four right angles.

c A _____ has two pairs of equal sides and four right angles.

d A _____ has only one pair of parallel sides.

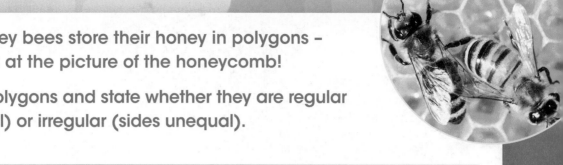

Task 2 Honey bees store their honey in polygons – look at the picture of the honeycomb!

Name these polygons and state whether they are regular (all sides equal) or irregular (sides unequal).

a _____

b _____

c _____

d _____

e What do you notice about the angles inside a regular polygon?

_____

f What do you notice about the angles inside an irregular polygon?

_____

Exploring Further ...

A   B   C   D

a i) What is the name of shape A? _____

ii) What two shapes are made by the dotted line on shape A?

_____ _____

b i) What is the name of shape B? _____

ii) What two shapes are made by the dotted line on shape B?

_____ _____

c i) What is the name of shape C? _____

ii) Draw a dotted line on shape C to make two trapeziums.

d i) What is the name of shape D? _____

ii) Draw a dotted line on shape D to make a rhombus and a kite.

Now buzz to pages 44–45 to record what you have learned in your explorer's logbook.

Circles

You need to be able to draw **circles** and you need to know the **properties** of circles.

Circumference

Diameter | Radius

Chord | Tangent

Arc

The diameter passes through the centre of the circle from one side to the other. It is twice the length of the radius. Make sure you also know what a circumference, chord, arc and tangent are.

Task 1 What is the diameter of a branch when the radius is?

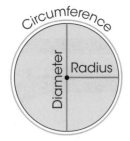

a 5 cm _____   b 4 cm _____   c 7 mm _____

What is the radius of a branch when the diameter is?

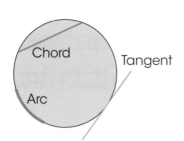

d 6 cm _____   e 14 mm _____   f 15 mm _____

34

Task 2

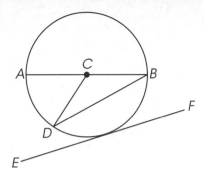

What do the following lines represent?

a AB _____

b CD _____

c BD _____

d EF _____

e AD (curved edge) _____

Task 3   Find the circumference of these circles. You can calculate the circumference of a circle by multiplying the diameter by 3.14

a Diameter of 2 cm _____   b Diameter of 5 cm _____

c Diameter of 6 cm _____   d Radius of 4 cm _____

e Radius of 2 cm _____   f Radius of 5 cm _____

Find the diameter of these circles.

g Circumference 12.56 cm _____   h Circumference 31.4 cm _____

i Circumference 28.26 cm _____   j Circumference 37.68 cm _____

Exploring Further ...

Make your own circle pattern on a separate piece of paper. Draw lots of intertwining circles with different diameters and colour your pattern.

Now race to pages 44–45 to record what you have learned in your explorer's logbook.

3D shapes

What can you remember about **3D shapes**?

- 3D shapes have 'bodies'.

- They have three dimensions: **length**, **width** and **height** (or depth).

- They can be described in terms of how many faces, edges and corners (vertices) they have.

- They can be opened up into a **net**. A net is a pattern of 2D shapes which can be cut out and folded to make a model of a 3D shape. There may be several possible nets for one 3D shape.

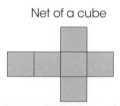

Net of a cube

Task 1 — Name each of these 3D shapes.

A	B	C	D	E	F	G	H

A = _____   B = _____   C = _____   D = _____   E = _____

F = _____

G = _____

H = _____

Task 2 Draw a line to match each net to the name of the shape.

A 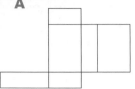 B   C   D 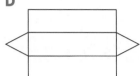 E

triangular prism   cuboid   cube   square-based pyramid   triangular-based pyramid

Task 3 Complete this net of a square-based pyramid. There are three possibilities.

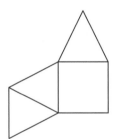   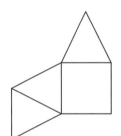   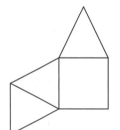

WILD FACT

There are over 1000 species of gall wasp. 70% of the known gall wasps live in various types of oak tree.

WILD FACT

Have you ever noticed strange spherical lumps on oak trees and other plants? They are called 'galls'. A gall is an abnormal swelling of the plant tissue. In oak trees the galls are also called oak apples. A gall is home to a tiny grub.

Exploring Further ...

The numbers on the opposite faces of a dice normally add up to seven, so 1 is opposite to 6, 5 to 2 and 3 to 4.

Put the missing numbers on these dice nets.

   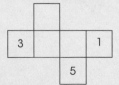   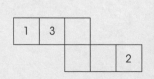

Now zip to pages 44–45 to record what you have learned in your explorer's logbook.

Coordinates

Coordinates are numbers which indicate a position on a graph or map. They usually come in pairs, e.g. (4, 5). The first number tells us the distance along and the second number tells us the distance up or down. Coordinates help us to describe the position of a shape. **Vectors**, e.g. $\binom{4}{5}$, are used to describe a **translation**. A translation occurs when a shape 'slides' to a new position without turning. The top figure shows how far the shape has moved along the *x*-axis. The bottom figure denotes movement along the *y*-axis.

FACT FILE

Animal: Hedgehog
Habitat: There are 15 species in Europe, Asia and Africa
Weight: 397 to 1106 g
Lifespan: 2 to 3 years
Diet: Insects, worms, centipedes, snails, mice, frogs and snakes

Task 1 **The following are three of the coordinates for various quadrilaterals. For each one predict the fourth coordinate.**

a **Square A:** (4, 7), (5, 5), (3, 4) ________

b **Rhombus B:** (–5, 3), (–3, 2), (–1, 3) ________

c **Rectangle C:** (–2, –3), (–2, –7), (–4, –7) ________

d **Parallelogram D:** (3, –2), (6, –2), (1, –4) ________

WILD FACT

A hedgehog has about 7000 spines on its body and there could be up to 500 fleas living amongst them!

WILD FACT

The hedgehog's fondness for slugs and snails makes it the gardener's friend.

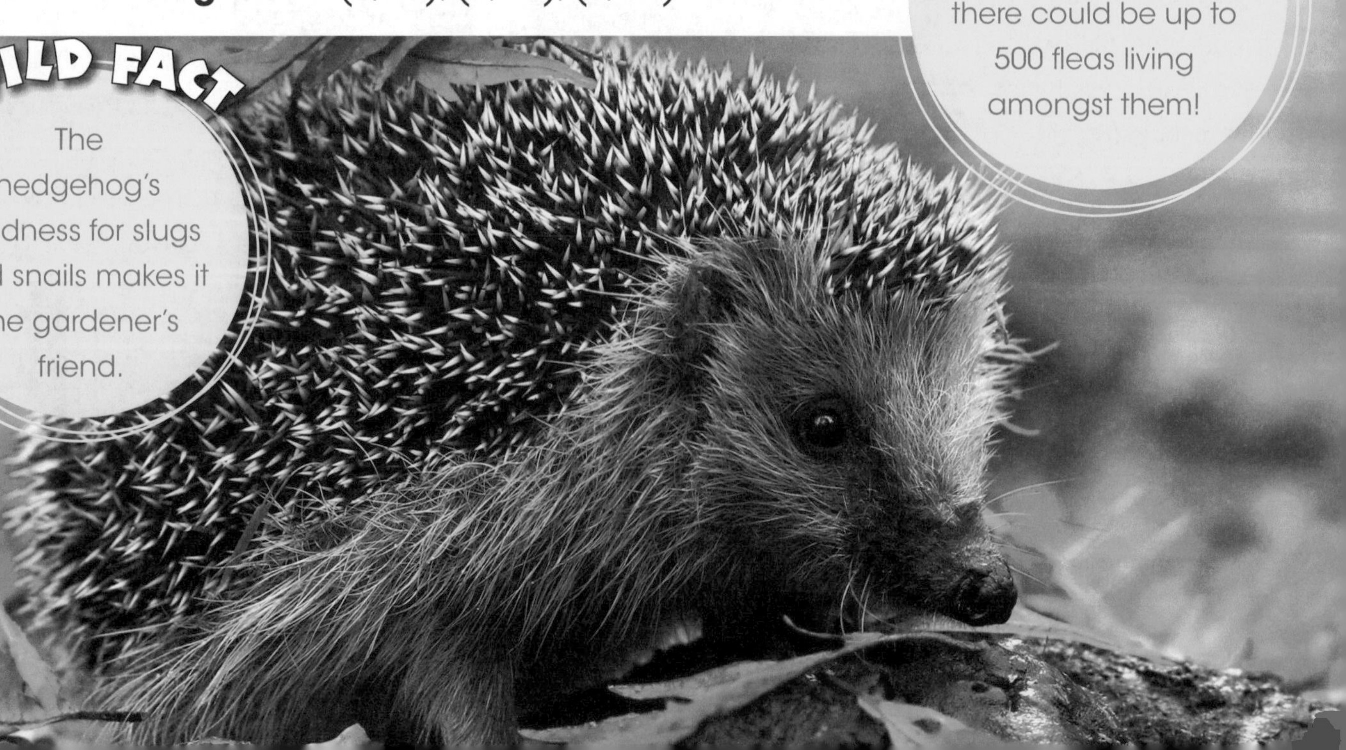

Task 2   Look at the positions of the shapes in the diagram.

a Translate square A by the vector $\binom{2}{-1}$. Label it B.

b Translate rectangle C by the vector $\binom{-3}{-1}$. Label it D.

c Reflect rhombus E in the x-axis. Label it F.

d Reflect parallelogram G in the y-axis. Label it H.

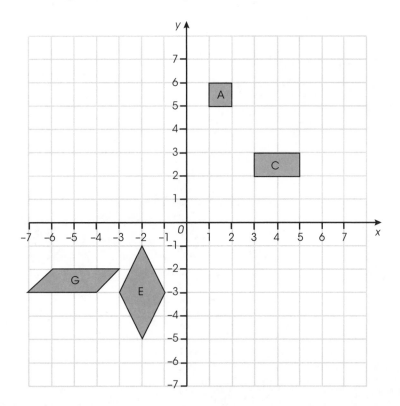

Exploring Further ...

This rectangle represents a garden where a hedgehog is searching for food. The coordinates of point D are (1, 5). The coordinates of point B are (4, 1).

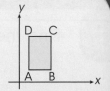

a The gardener has left some dog food at point A.

What are the coordinates of point A? _____

b At C there is a log pile where the hedgehog will find lots of slugs.

Give the coordinates of point C. _____

c The neighbour's garden is a reflection of this one in the x-axis. Give the coordinates of the neighbour's garden.

A _____   B _____   C _____   D _____

Now shuffle to pages 44–45 to record what you have learned in your explorer's logbook.

Statistics

The pine marten is related to the stoat and the weasel. It is distinguished by its long bushy tail.

Scientists collect all sorts of **data** (information) about our wildlife. The data can then be analysed to look for significant trends and changes. Investigate two ways of displaying information here with the **pie chart** and the **line graph**.

One way of analysing results is finding the **mean**. The mean gives the **average** or central value of a set of results. To find the mean, add up all the figures and divide the sum by the number of figures you added.

FACT FILE

Animal:	Pine marten
Habitat:	Woodland, mainly coniferous
Weight:	1 to 2.5 kg
Lifespan:	Up to 10 years
Diet:	The flesh of dead animals, plus small mammals, birds, eggs, invertebrates, fruits and nuts

Task 1   Find the mean values (averages).

a Over the course of five nights, I saw 9, 12, 6, 13 and 10 bats flying over the reservoir. What was the mean value for the five nights?

_____

b A pine marten was tagged to see how far it travelled each night. Over six nights it travelled 3 km, $1\frac{1}{2}$ km, 3 km, 2 km, 3 km and $2\frac{1}{2}$ km. What was the average distance travelled per night?

_____

Task 2 — This pie chart shows the diet of a pine marten.

a Which two foods form the main part of the pine marten's diet?

_____ _____

Food

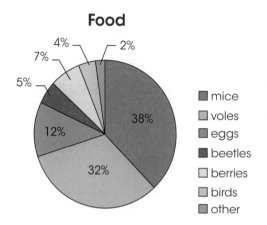

- mice
- voles
- eggs
- beetles
- berries
- birds
- other

4% 2% 7% 5% 12% 38% 32%

b What percentage of the diet is eggs?

_____

c What percentage of the diet is berries?

_____

d Do eggs, beetles, berries and birds together form a bigger part of the diet than mice? Explain your answer.

_____

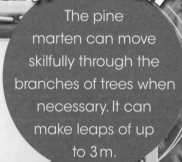

WILD FACT

The pine marten can move skilfully through the branches of trees when necessary. It can make leaps of up to 3 m.

Exploring Further ...

This line graph compares the numbers of three species of butterfly recorded at a nature reserve over a seven-year period.

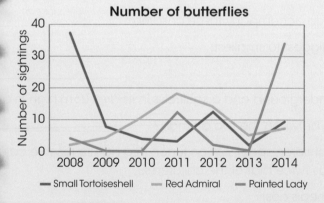

Number of butterflies

Number of sightings

40 30 20 10 0

2008 2009 2010 2011 2012 2013 2014

— Small Tortoiseshell — Red Admiral — Painted Lady

a In which year was the number of Small Tortoiseshell butterflies at its highest? _____

b In which years were there no sightings of the Painted Lady?

_____ _____ _____

c In 2011, which species of butterfly was seen the most?

_____

Now leap to pages 44–45 to record what you have learned in your explorer's logbook.

Quick test

Now try these questions. Give yourself 1 mark for every correct answer - but only if you answer each part of the question correctly.

1   Order these deer according to their weight, starting with the heaviest:
    Red   one hundred and eighty thousand four hundred and ninety-one grams
    Muntjac   15 249 g
    Sika   one hundred and nine thousand nine hundred and twelve grams
    Roe   33 489 g

    _____   ☐

2   Here is a breakdown of the numbers of urban foxes in England:
    London 9649; Birmingham 3208; Manchester 6753; Bristol 3529; Liverpool 2876; Other areas 3492

    What is the total population of urban foxes in England?   _____   ☐

3   The total fox population in England is 270 000. Use your answer to
    question 2 to calculate how many foxes are living in rural areas. _____   ☐

4   Look at these numbers: 44, 17, 47, 90, 63, 97, 67, 35, 14, 25, 64, 42
    a   Which number is a multiple of?

        i   2, 4 and 8 _____   **ii**   3, 7 and 9   _____   ☐

    b   Which are the four prime numbers?   _____

5   160 hibernacula were identified. It was estimated that each hibernaculum contained 40 adders.   ☐

    How many adders were there in total?   _____

6   Visitors to a bird reserve recorded on average 37 sightings of different birds each day.
    This number was calculated by dividing the total number of sightings in a year by 365.

    What was the total number of sightings recorded in the year?   _____   ☐

7   A school visit was organised for 264 children. One adult was required for every ten children.   ☐

    How many adults were needed to accompany these children? _____

8   Put these values in order from biggest to smallest:

    $\frac{7}{35}$, 0.25, 21%   ☐

    _____

9   A fox is resting in its den 2.5 m underground and a squirrel is in its drey 26 m high in a pine tree.   ☐

    What is the difference in metres between the two animals?   _____

10 A family of two adults and two children spent £24 on lunch in a nature reserve café.
    The cost of the adults' meals was twice that of the children's.

    How much did the two adults' meals cost?   _____   ☐

11 On a hiking holiday, a family walked 87 km in 6 days. Assuming that they walked the
    same distance each day, how far would they walk in 8 days?

    _____   ☐

12 Sort these shapes into the table below. Put each shape into as many boxes as appropriate.

    A   B   C   D   E   F

Two Pairs of Equal Sides	All Sides Equal	At Least One Pair of Parallel Sides	At Least One Right Angle	One or More Pairs of Opposite Angles Which are Equal

☐

13 The three angles of a triangle are *x*, *y* and *z*.
$x + y = 126°$ $143° - z = y$
What is the value of each angle?   *x* = _____ *y* = _____ *z* = _____

14 This is the net of a cuboid.
Mark the edge which will
join A when the net is folded
into a cuboid.

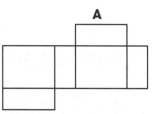

15 Complete the square
in the upper right-hand
quadrant of this grid,
labelling the third and
fourth points *C* and *D*
and giving the
coordinates of all
four points.

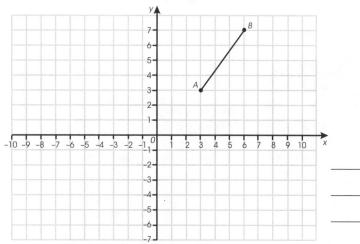

_____

_____

_____

_____

16 Reflect the completed square in question 15 in the line $x = 2$.

Give the coordinates of the reflected square. _____

17 This graph shows the rainfall at
Green Moss Nature Reserve on
two consecutive weeks.

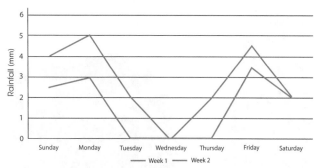

Giving your answers to 2 decimal places, calculate the mean daily rainfall for:

a week 1 _____   **b** week 2 _____

18 One pair of swallows fed their chicks a total of 23 424 meals during June and July.

On average, how many meals did they feed their chicks each day? _____

19 Calculate the size of the
angles marked with a letter.

x = _____ *y* = _____

20 Fred needs wood to build some hedgehog houses. He needs ten 30 cm pieces.
He is prepared to cut the pieces to get the cheapest deal. Which shop should he buy from?
Mike Deer and Son: 4 m lengths cost £12.40 each
Martin Pine Supplies: 60 cm lengths cost £2.49 each
S. Wallow Ltd: 900 mm lengths cost £3.12 each   _____

How did you do?   1-5 Try again   6-10 Good try!

11-15 Great work!   **16-20 Excellent exploring!**   **/20**

Explorer's Logbook

Tick off the topics as you complete them and then colour in the star.

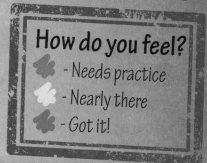
Ordering numbers ☐

Area and perimeter ☐

Multiples and factors ☐

Long multiplication ☐

Angles in triangles ☐

Problem solving ☐

Standard measures ☐

Decimals ☐

Coordinates ☐

Ratio and proportion ☐

Algebra ☐

Fractions ☐

Circles ☐

Volume ☐

3D shapes ☐

Polygons ☐

Addition and subtraction ☐

Division ☐

Percentages ☐

Statistics ☐

45

Answers

Pages 2–3

Task 1

a six million four hundred and four thousand three hundred and twenty

b nine million and fifteen   **c** 10 000 000   **d** 5 000 002

Task 2

a 4 300 990   4 034 003   4 033 999
   3 444 004   3 434 777

b 8   4   −1   −2   −9

Task 3

a ten million   **b** ten thousand   **c** one hundred
d one thousand **e** one hundred thousand **f** one unit

Exploring Further …

	M	HTh	TTh	Th	H	T	U	
a	2	0	5	6	0	7	0	E
b						1	8	R
c			4	0	0	0	0	D
d	4	0	0	0	0	0	0	D
e						1	8	R
f		5	0	0	0	0	0	E
g	3	9	5	9	6	8	1	E

h Red deer

Pages 4–5

Task 1

a 19 948   **b** 689 589   **c** 2341   **d** 232 665

Task 2

a 2446   **b** 30 100   **c** 6102   **d** 102 862

Task 3

a 96 919   **b** 1 107 794   **c** 13 611   **d** 186 883

Exploring Further …

46 257 + 57 889 + 19 005 = 123 151
1 000 875 − 123 151 = 877 724
877 724 birds arrived safely.

Pages 6–7

Task 1

a i) 8, 12, 16   ii) 80, 120, 160   iii) 800, 1200, 1600
b i) 22, 33, 44   ii) 220, 330, 440   iii) 2200, 3300, 4400
c i) 14, 21, 28   ii) 140, 210, 280   iii) 1400, 2100, 2800

Task 2

a 2, 3, 4, 6, 8, 9, 12, 18, 24, 36
b 2, 3, 6, 7, 14, 21
c 72: 1 and 72   42: 1 and 42

Task 3

a 1 and 7   **b** 40   **c** 80

Exploring Further …

a 3, 13, 23, 43, 53, 73, 83, 103, 113 are prime numbers.
b The lowest factors of the remaining numbers are:
   33:   3   63:   3   93:   3
   123: 3   133: 7   143: 11
   153: 3

Pages 8–9

Task 1

a 690   **b** 280   **c** 1790   **d** 3610

Task 2

a 3360   **b** 1770   **c** 5860   **d** 63 540

Task 3

a 6045   **b** 2054   **c** 18 396
d 29 750   **e** 55 290   **f** 266 892

Task 4

a 80 × 70 = 5600 **b** 30 × 30 = 900
c 30 × 50 = 1500 **d** 400 × 80 = 32 000

Exploring Further …

a The most efficient estimate is
   (3000 × 50) + (3500 × 50) = 325 000
b 2875 × 48 = 138 000
   3485 × 52 = 181 220
   138 000 + 181 220 = 319 220

Pages 10–11

Task 1

a 96   **b** 82   **c** 971   **d** 163

Task 2

a 6   **b** 8   **c** 6   **d** 13

Task 3

a i) 1571 r4   ii) $1571\frac{4}{5}$ iii) 1571.8

b i) 2346 r3   ii) $2346\frac{3}{4}$ iii) 2346.75

c i) 1209 r2   ii) $1209\frac{1}{4}$ iii) 1209.25

Task 4

a 109 r34   **b** $146\frac{1}{4}$

Exploring Further …

a 9700 ÷ 27 = 359 r7.   359 complete trays
b 20 more plants
c 8 journeys

Pages 12–13

Task 1

a 13 + 16 ÷ 2 **(÷ first)** = 13 + 8 = 21
b 5 × 3 + 2 × 4 − 12 ÷ 4 **(× & ÷ first)**
   = 15 + 8 − 3 = 20
c 8 × 3 + 9 ÷ 3 − 8 **(× & ÷ first)** = 24 + 3 − 8 = 19
d 35 − (15 + 5 × 3) **(brackets first, within the brackets × first)**
   = 35 − (15 + 15) = 35 − 30 = 5

Task 2

a $(4 + 2)^2 + 3 × 2 − 2^2$ **(brackets first)** $= 6^2 + 3 × 2 − 2^2$ **(now orders)** = 36 + 3 × 2 − 4 **(now ×)** = 38
b $(12 ÷ 2 + 8) − (5^2 − 3 × 7)$
   = (6 + 8) − (25 − 21) = 14 − 4 = 10
c $(4^2 + 2 − 6) ÷ (3^2 + 7 − 7 × 2)$ = (16 + 2 − 6)
   ÷ (9 + 7 − 14) = 12 ÷ 2 = 6
d $(3^3 ÷ 3 × 2) − 2^3$ = (27 ÷ 3 × 2) − 8 = 18 − 8 = 10

Task 3

a 143 cm + 62 cm = 205 cm
   260 cm − 205 cm = 55 cm
   The fourth adder measures 55 cm.
b 617 + 29 = 646 pairs of hen harriers in 2010
   770 + 36 = 806 pairs of hen harriers in 2004
   806 − 646 = 160 fewer pairs in 2010 than in 2004
   160 × 2 = 320 birds
   In the **6** years from 2004 to 2010, the total number of hen harriers in the UK and the Isle of Man fell by **320**.

Task 4

a 359 + 451 + 1349 = 2159 km
   3902 − 2159 = 1743 km
   The fourth leg was 1743 km.
b 3902 km × 57 = 222 414 km

Exploring Further …

The fallow deer and roe deer together weigh:
236 − 119 = 117 kg
First take away the 47 kg difference: 117 − 47 = 70 kg
To find the weight of the roe deer, halve this so the roe deer weighs: 70 ÷ 2 = 35 kg

Now add 35 to 47 so the fallow deer weighs:
35 + 47 = 82 kg
Check your calculations:
82 − 35 = 47 kg
119 + 82 + 35 = 236 kg

Pages 14–15
Task 1
a i) HCF = 3 $\frac{9}{12} = \frac{3}{4}$ ii) HCF = 2 $\frac{2}{20} = \frac{1}{10}$

   iii) HCF = 4 $\frac{8}{12} = \frac{2}{3}$ iv) HCF = 6 $\frac{12}{18} = \frac{2}{3}$

b i) HCF = 5 $\frac{25}{60} = \frac{5}{12}$ ii) HCF = 3 $\frac{24}{33} = \frac{8}{11}$

   iii) HCF = 7 $\frac{35}{42} = \frac{5}{6}$ iv) HCF = 9 $\frac{36}{81} = \frac{4}{9}$

c 24   d 42

Task 2
a $\frac{7}{8} = \frac{21}{24}$ $\frac{2}{3} = \frac{16}{24}$ $\frac{11}{12} = \frac{22}{24}$ $\frac{2}{3}, \frac{7}{8}, \frac{11}{12}$

b $\frac{13}{18} = \frac{26}{36}$ $\frac{5}{9} = \frac{20}{36}$ $\frac{7}{12} = \frac{21}{36}$ $\frac{5}{9}, \frac{7}{12}, \frac{13}{18}$

Task 3
a i) $1\frac{1}{16}$ ii) $1\frac{1}{3}$ b i) $\frac{3}{10}$ ii) $\frac{2}{9}$ c i) $5\frac{7}{9}$ ii) $7\frac{27}{28}$

Task 4
a i) $\frac{1}{5}$ ii) $\frac{1}{12}$ b i) 6 ii) 28   c i) $\frac{1}{8}$ ii) $\frac{1}{14}$

Exploring Further …
$\frac{21}{35} = \frac{3}{5}$ $\frac{18}{48} = \frac{3}{8}$ $\frac{21}{33} = \frac{7}{11}$

$\frac{15}{35} = \frac{3}{7}$ $\frac{24}{54} = \frac{4}{9}$ $\frac{30}{72} = \frac{5}{12}$

Pages 16–17
Task 1
a three thousand   b three thousandths
c three units   d three hundred

Task 2
a i) 570   ii) 9364   b i) 0.124   ii) 1.975
c i) 3570   ii) 4   d i) 0.507   ii) 81.529

Task 3
a 0.85   b 0.875   c $0.\dot{5}$ d $0.58\dot{3}$

Task 4
a 7.35   b 30.54   c 4.8   d 172.25

Exploring Further …
Area 1: 37   Area 2: 86   Area 3: 24   Area 4: 119

Pages 18–19
Task 1
a $\frac{71}{100}$ b $\frac{3}{100}$ c $\frac{25}{100} = \frac{1}{4}$ d $\frac{50}{100} = \frac{1}{2}$

Task 2
a 0.91   b 2.56   c 0.08   d 0.01
e 12%   f 37%   g 5%   h 361%

Task 3
a 99%   b 9%   c 80%   d 95%

Task 4
a i) 4   ii) 16   iii) 38
b i) 2   ii) 8   iii) 19
c i) 6   ii) 24   iii) 57

Exploring Further …
$\frac{4}{5}$ = 80% = 0.8 $\frac{7}{10}$ = 70% = 0.7 $\frac{3}{20}$ = 15% = 0.15

$\frac{1}{4}$ = 25% = 0.25 $\frac{7}{20}$ = 35% = 0.35 $\frac{41}{50}$ = 82% = 0.82

$\frac{3}{10}$ = 30% = 0.3 $\frac{13}{25}$ = 52% = 0.52 $\frac{1}{25}$ = 4% = 0.04

Pages 20–21
Task 1
a 12 g b 36 g c £9 d 90 p e £13.50 f £2.70

Task 2
a $\frac{1}{2}$ cm (0.5 cm)   b 2 cm

c $2\frac{1}{4}$ cm (2.25 cm)   d 560 km

e 80 km   f 120 km

Task 3
a $\frac{9}{10}$ b 4 c 40 d 1:9 e 10% f 90%

Exploring Further …
Sparrow: 8, 24, $\frac{24}{60}$, $\frac{2}{5}$, 40%, 0.4

Starling: 6, 18, $\frac{18}{60}$, $\frac{3}{10}$, 30%, 0.3

Blackbird: 3, 9, $\frac{9}{60}$, $\frac{3}{20}$, 15%, 0.15

Wren: 2, 6, $\frac{6}{60}$, $\frac{1}{10}$, 10%, 0.1

Robin: 1, 3, $\frac{3}{60}$, $\frac{1}{20}$, 5%, 0.05

TOTAL: 20, 60, $\frac{60}{60}$, 1 whole, 100%, 1.0

Pages 22–23
Task 1
a 30, 26, 22   b 26, 33, 41   c −1, −3, −5

Task 2
a 480 486 492 498 504 510
b −12 −7 −2 3 8 13
c Subtract 99   d Add 1, then 2, then 3, etc.

Task 3
a i) x = 58   ii) y = 22   iii) z = 21
b i) a = 24   ii) b = 43   iii) c = 107
c i) p = 72   ii) q = 7   iii) r = 6
d i) k = 9   ii) m = 2   iii) n = 42

Task 4
a Any two of the following:
   x = 11, y = 0   x = 7, y = 4   x = 3, y = 8
   x = 10, y = 1   x = 6 y = 5   x = 2, y = 9
   x = 9, y = 2   x = 5, y = 6   x = 1, y = 10
   x = 8, y = 3   x = 4, y = 7   x = 0, y = 11

b Any two of the following:
   p = 12, q = 1   p = 4, q = 3   p = 2, q = 6
   p = 6, q = 2   p = 3, q = 4   p = 1, q = 12

c c = 4   d c = 2

Exploring Further …

	Distance (m)	Time (min)	Speed (m/min)	Speed (km/h)
Red deer	2400	3	800	48
Kingfisher	900	$1\frac{1}{2}$	600	36
Swallow	600	$\frac{2}{3}$	900	54

The swallow is the fastest.

Pages 24–25
Task 1
a Red deer   2.75 m   120 kg
b Harvest mouse   50 mm   5.1 g
c Red fox   112 cm   5.9 kg
d Squirrel   25 cm   0.71 kg

Task 2
a 700 kg b 80 cm c 0.16 t d 0.3 litres e 3 miles

Task 3
a i) 324 s   ii) 105 s
b i) 24.5 days   ii) 61 days
c 18 min   d 7 min 30 s

Exploring Further …
i) 5 day   ii) 8 km   iii) 4 hours
iv) 300 cm or 3 m   v) 15 kg   vi) 40 cm
vii) 4 g   viii) 4 cm or 40 mm

Pages 26–27
Task 1
a True   b False   c False   d True   e True

Task 2
a 43°   **b** 42° and 48°   **c** 40°

Task 3
a scalene   **b** equilateral
c right angled   **d** isosceles

Exploring Further …
a Triangle B
b All three sides are equal and all three angles are equal.

Pages 28–29
Task 1
a i) 2000 mm³   ii) 3500 mm³
b i) 4 cm³   ii) 1 000 000 cm³
c i) 4 000 000 cm³   ii) 2 500 000 cm³
d i) 3 m³   ii) 1.5 m³

Task 2
a 48 cm³   **b** 60 m³   **c** 112 mm³
d 120 cm³   **e** 48 m³   **f** 160 mm³

Task 3
a i) 24 cm² 18 cm² 12 cm²   ii) 72 cm³
b 12 × 5 × 4 = 240 cm³
Weight of each cube = 7.2 ÷ 240 = 0.03 kg = 30 g
c i) 4 × 6 × 9 = 216 m³
216 m³ = 216 000 kg
221 000 kg − 216 000 kg = 5000 kg
The weight of the tank is 5000 kg.
ii) 216 m³ = 216 000 litres
The tank holds 216 000 litres of water.

Exploring Further …
The volume of one small box of pamphlets
= 15 × 5 × 4 = 300 cm³
The volume of the large box
= 60 × 20 × 16 = 19 200 cm³

$\frac{1}{4}$ of this volume = 19 200 ÷ 4 = 4800 cm³

$\frac{3}{4}$ of this volume = 4800 × 3 = 14 400 cm³

14 400 ÷ 300 = 48
The large box will hold 48 small boxes.

Pages 30–31
Task 1
a i) 20 m²   ii) 18 m   **b** i) 25 cm²   ii) 20 cm
c i) 5202 m²   ii) 374 m   **d** i) 64 m²   ii) 32 m
e i) 72 cm²   ii) 36 cm   **f** i) 576 mm²   ii) 96 mm

Task 2
Area = 96 cm²
Perimeter = 56 cm

Task 3
a 12 cm²   **b** 3 cm   **c** 32 cm²   **d** 9 cm

Exploring Further …
Triangles A and B and parallelogram *CDEF* share the same height. By substituting appropriate values for *a* and *b*, you will discover that:
a The area of A is twice the area of B.
b The area of parallelogram *CDEF* is twice the area of triangles A and B added together.

Pages 32–33
Task 1
a kite   **b** square   **c** rectangle   **d** trapezium

Task 2
a regular pentagon   **b** irregular octagon
c irregular quadrilateral   **d** regular hexagon
e They are equal.
f They are not equal.

Exploring Further …
a i) parallelogram   ii) triangle and trapezium
b i) (irregular) pentagon   ii) triangle and rectangle

c i) (regular) hexagon   **d** i) (irregular) hexagon
ii)   ii)

Pages 34–35
Task 1
a 10 cm   **b** 8 cm   **c** 14 mm   **d** 3 cm   **e** 7 mm   **f** 7.5 mm

Task 2
a *AB* = diameter   **b** *CD* = radius   **c** *BD* = chord
d *EF* = tangent   **e** *AD* = arc

Task 3
a 6.28 cm   **b** 15.7 cm   **c** 18.84 cm   **d** 25.12 cm
e 12.56 cm   **f** 31.4 cm   **g** 4 cm   **h** 10 cm
i 9 cm   **j** 12 cm

Pages 36–37
Task 1
A = cube   **B** = cuboid   **C** = sphere
D = cylinder   **E** = cone   **F** = triangular prism
G = square-based pyramid   **H** = triangular-based pyramid

Task 2
A = cuboid   **B** = cube   **C** = triangular-based pyramid
D = triangular prism   **E** = square-based pyramid

Task 3

Exploring Further …

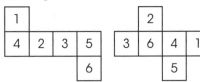

Pages 38–39
Task 1
a (2, 6)   **b** (−3, 4)   **c** (−4, −3)   **d** (4, −4)

Task 2
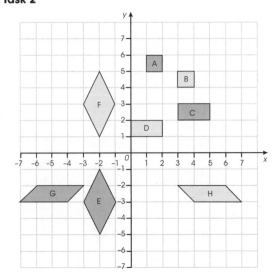